Stand-up Paddleboarding

by K. C. Kelley

Published by The Child's World®
1980 Lookout Drive
Mankato, MN 56003-1705
800-599-READ
www.childsworld.com

The Child's World®: Mary Berendes, Publishing Director
Shoreline Publishing Group, LLC: James Buckley Jr.,
    Production Director
The Design Lab: Design and production

ISBN: 978-1-60973-179-3
LCCN: 2011928871

Photo credits: Cover: dreamstime.com/paparico.
Interior: Corbis: 11, 19, 23; dreamstime.com: Paparico
4, Paul Topp 8, AJ Photos 12, Jeffrey Walthall 20;
Mike Eliason: 7, 28; Getty Images: 24; iStock: 15, 16;
Photo courtesy of Paddle Surf Hawaii: 27.

Printed in the United States of America
Mankato, Minnesota
July, 2011
PA02094

Table of Contents

Surfing and paddling meet
in this hot new sport.

4

CHAPTER ONE

What's SUP?

The sun sparkles off a crystal-blue ocean. The breeze is warm, just right for lounging on the sand. As you relax on your towel, you notice something moving in the water just off the beach.

It's a person . . . but he seems to be standing on the water! This is no miracle, however. You see that he's standing on a long board. Must be a surfer, you think. Surfers ride boards to catch waves on which they do tricks and turns.

Two things, however, catch your eye. The first is that there are no waves today. The ocean in front of you is flat calm, with tiny **wavelets** lapping the shore. So how could he be surfing?

The second is that this surfer is carrying a paddle.

A paddle? What's going on here?

You've just discovered SUP: stand-up paddleboarding, the hottest new sport in the water.

Since about 2000, the sport of SUP has jumped in popularity. It's not surfing and it's not kayaking; it's a blend of both. Riders stand on long, heavy boards and use a long paddle to move through the water. The sport takes a lot of balance. It can be done in flat water or through surf.

Because you use your arms, legs, and **torso** to balance and paddle, SUP is a great full-body workout. Many people who have never surfed enjoy SUP. It gets them out on the water while also providing good work for their muscles.

One of the biggest reasons SUP has become so popular is that you don't need waves to try it. SUP works just as well on flat bays, rivers, or lakes as it does on the rolling ocean.

Arms, legs, and body all get a workout when stand-up paddling.

Waikiki Beach in Hawaii fills with people who want to play in the warm Pacific Ocean.

Surfing has been around for centuries. Ancient South Pacific islanders used long wooden boards to catch waves off their islands. The English explorer Capt. James Cook wrote about seeing surfers during his **voyages** in the 1700s. The islanders also used long, flat canoes. Sometimes they had to stand to paddle the canoes through shallow water.

From what historians can find, these islanders didn't really combine surfing and paddling. That was left to some beach-loving Hawaiians in the 1950s. In those years after World War II, tourists flocked to Waikiki Beach on Oahu. They wanted to try out surfing. Local surfers known as "beach boys" figured out that they could snap photos of the tourists surfing. They sold the photos as souvenirs. The best way to take a photo while riding a board was to carry a paddle to help keep upright and moving. SUP, or "beach boy surfing," as it's sometimes called, was born.

The sport stayed quiet and local until about 2000, when international surf star Laird Hamilton and other pro surfers rediscovered it. They found that they could SUP to get a great workout on days when there was not much surf. Once they tried that, they tried the boards in waves, too. The long paddles helped them carve tight turns, even though the boards were long and heavy.

With the publicity of these stars, the sport grew rapidly. Almost unknown in the 1990s, by 2009, there were two international SUP pro tours. Thousands of people have tried this new sport, and SUP rentals are found on beaches everywhere.

Let's find out how you can get up from that towel next time you're at the beach. Or should we say, how you can stand-up . . . and paddle!

Punting in England

Standing up and paddling is not limited to boards. In England, people stand while paddling narrow river boats called "punts." They have a very small draft, which means they have a flat bottom that doesn't go deep into the water. Punts are perfect for small rivers and canals. They don't work well in oceans or deep water, however.

Laird Hamilton shows off his paddle-surf form.

Stand-up paddleboards
are very long. This makes
them more stable.

12

CHAPTER TWO

Start by Standing

The first thing you need is the board. Stand-up paddle boards are made of a strong material that floats very well. There's no danger of sinking. The boards have a flat top and a slightly rounded underside. At the back on the bottom is a small fin or pair of fins. This helps the board balance once you're on it.

Beginners use a board that is about 10 feet (3 m) long and 34 inches (86 cm) wide. Boards come in longer and shorter sizes as well. Riders looking to catch more waves will probably choose a shorter board. Those heading out for long, flat rides like a longer board.

Depending on the board you ride, you might add wax. This coating is rubbed on the top of the board and helps your feet get a good grip.

It's easier to balance yourself while kneeling down.
Start this way to get a feel for riding on the board.

To start stand-up paddling, get on your knees. Sounds odd, right? But you can't just step out of the water onto the board. The best way is to place the paddle across the board. Then, holding the paddle and a side of the board, lift or hop up so that you're kneeling on the board. Try to be at the center of the board, both from side to side and end to end. Take a few strokes and feel how the board balances.

When you're comfortable on your knees, try standing, one foot at a time. A good paddling position is with the toes pointed forward and the knees slightly bent. Stand-up straight, not hunched over. Try to look out in front of you. Looking down at your feet can upset your balance.

The best way to paddle is to place your top hand over the handle of the paddle. Your bottom hand holds the pole and slides up and down as you paddle. Most paddles have a slight bend in them. Point the paddle so that the very bottom of the paddle points away from you, not toward you.

Reach forward with paddle into the water and pull back alongside the board. Pull back about as far as your feet. Pull smoothly and evenly, not hard and fast. By paddling on one side and then the other, you keep it going straight. When paddling, twist your body as you pull to get the most power.

If you want to turn, you have a couple of ways to go. The easiest way is to paddle more on one side. You'll turn in the direction opposite direction. You can also hold the paddle in the water and drag it along the back of the board. That will turn the nose, or front, of the board to the side you're dragging.

Using long, slow strokes on flat water, you can
find yourself paddling out to incredible views.

SPLASH!

Yes, you will fall off your board. It happens to the best of them. Here are a couple of key tips:

- If you feel yourself falling, aim for the water instead of the board. You'll just get wet if you hit the water. You might bonk your head if you hit the board.
- Once in the water, swim to the board first. Climb on and kneel down. Paddle with your hands to get to the paddle itself.

Surfriders steer their boards just as if they're riding a boat.

For more expert riders, SUP in the waves is an awesome treat. Knowing how to surf first will make this much easier. It's not for SUP beginners . . . but it sure is fun!

For catching waves, you'll use a SUP board that's shorter and narrower. This makes turning with either paddle or feet easier. A smaller paddle also helps you make lots of quick, short strokes so you can get up speed to ride the wave.

Once you're on the wave, the foot position is different. Instead of toes forward, your toes will point mostly toward one side of the board. This helps you control it with your feet as well as with the paddle. Paddle surfers on waves often use their paddle like a boat uses a **rudder**. They hold it in the water behind them to help steer their board.

CHAPTER THREE

Super SUP Stories

Though beach boys in Waikiki did it first, Laird Hamilton is really the one who helped put SUP on the world water map. His experiments with long boards came while helping his daughters learn to surf. Then he added a paddle of his own design, and bingo—a new sport.

Hamilton is world-famous for surfing the biggest waves in the world. He was one of the first to have a Jet Ski tow him into giant waves. For for all of his adventures on the water, he picks one sport as his favorite.

"If I could do just one thing on the water, I'd pick stand-up paddleboard," Hamilton told ABC News. "I can ride giant waves, small waves, or even paddle on a river. For me, it's like dancing on the water."

He's not kidding. In 2006, Hamilton paddled across the English Channel (26.7 miles/43 km) in six hours. He says one of his dreams is to paddle-surf in a hurricane!

Laird Hamilton can ride the big waves—with or without a paddle!

David Kalama is a star on the growing pro SUP tour.

Other top watermen and women have joined Hamilton in loving SUP. With all these new athletes in this new sport, competing was the natural move. In 2009, the International Surfing Association started a world championship of distance and surfing events. The first pro series in the United States is beginning in 2011 through the World Paddle Association (WPA).

One of the biggest events is in Hawaii, the sport's home. The Naish Paddle Open is named for Robby Naish, a windsurfing champion. It's held off Kahului Beach on Maui. Paddlers go 9.5 miles (15.3 km) along the shoreline through waves and wind. The 2010 winner, David Kalama, completed the course in 1 hour and 13 minutes. Longer races are held between the Hawaiian islands.

Races are held all over Hawaii, in Florida, North Carolina, and California. Events on lakes can be found in places like Lake Tahoe on the California-Nevada border, and on lakes in Oregon.

Pro sports usually need a group to organize them. SUP is no different. Several groups have been started to create events and rankings. In 2009, the Stand Up World Tour began with several events. The WPA holds contests around the world, too.

In 2010, Kurt Byron was the top-ranked racer in WPA, followed by Dane Morrissey. They racked up the most points at more than dozen WPA events.

Also in 2010, Hawaiian Kai Lenny won the 2010 Stand Up World Tour Championship with a victory at the final event, which was held in his home state. Kai is only 19, so figures to be a big name in the sport for years to come.

Women are just coming into the top competing ranks. One name to watch is Tiffany Paglinawan from Hawaii. She got a lot of attention for her attempts at paddle surfing the famous Pipeline **break** off Oahu.

World Record
In 2008, a Florida paddler named Justin DeBree went 420 miles (675.9 km) to set a world record for the longest SUP ride. He was raising money to fight skin cancer. He was on the board for almost 24 hours!

Tiffany Paglinawan took her surfing skills with her when she jumped to paddle-surfing.

Flat water and beautiful scenery make beaches great places to stand-up paddle.

If you're just looking for a nice day on the board, the beaches of the U.S. offer hundreds of places to SUP. One of the best is Santa Barbara, California. It's home to one of the first all-SUP shops in the nation. Protected by offshore islands, the city's bay offers long, flat places to paddle. And the scenery onshore and off can't be beat.

Many Florida beaches also offer SUP rentals; those on the Gulf of Mexico side might be better as they have less surf. Don't forget lakes and slow-moving rivers, either.

SUP is growing in popularity anywhere that land meets water. You get a great workout, a new view of the ocean or lake, and you have a lot of fun, too. It's much better than just lying on that beach towel. Get up and walk on the water!

Glossary

break—a place just offshore where large waves crash

flotation—the ability to float on water

rudder—an underwater blade that helps control direction of water vessels

torso—the central part of the human body, including the chest and abdomen

voyages—long trips

wavelets—tiny waves of water

Find Out More

BOOKS

The Stand Up Paddle Book
By Nate Burgoyne. Honolulu: Lava Rock Publishing, 2010.
This book is aimed at older readers, but it's still packed with lots of great SUP information.

Surfing
By K.C. Kelley. Mankato, MN: The Child's World, 2011.
Find out more about SUP's action sports cousin, the high-action world of surfing.

WEB SITES

For links to learn more about extreme sports: **childsworld.com/links**

Note to Parents, Teachers, and Librarians: We routinely verify our Web links to make sure they are safe and active sites. So encourage your readers to check them out!

Index

About the Author

K.C. Kelley loves watching paddleboarders and surfers at the beach near his house in Santa Barbara, California. He has also written books about baseball, football, and soccer, as well as about animals, astronauts, and other cool stuff.